BOLDLY COMES JUSTICE

Abhijit Naskar is the twenty-first century Neuroscientist whose contributions in Cognitive and Behavioral Neuroscience continue to aid human struggle against mental illness, prejudice, hate, extremism, discrimination and segregation. As an untiring advocate of mental health and universal acceptance, he became a beloved best-selling author all over the world with his very first book "The Art of Neuroscience in Everything". With his pioneering ventures into the Neuropsychology of beliefs and biases, he has hugely contributed in the eradication of religious and cultural differences in our world, for which he is popularly hailed as a humanitarian scientist, who takes the human civilization in the path of sweet general harmony.

BOLDLY COMES JUSTICE

SENTIENT NOT SILENT

ABHIJIT NASKAR

Also by Abhijit Naskar

The Art of Neuroscience in Everything
Your Own Neuron: A Tour of Your Psychic Brain
The God Parasite: Revelation of Neuroscience
The Spirituality Engine
Love Sutra: The Neuroscientific Manual of Love
Homo: A Brief History of Consciousness
Neurosutra: The Abhijit Naskar Collection
Autobiography of God: Biopsy of A Cognitive Reality
Biopsy of Religions: Neuroanalysis towards Universal
Tolerance
Prescription: Treating India's Soul
What is Mind?
In Search of Divinity: Journey to The Kingdom of Conscience
Love, God & Neurons: Memoir of a scientist who found
himself by getting lost
The Islamophobic Civilization: Voyage of Acceptance
Neurons of Jesus: Mind of A Teacher, Spouse & Thinker
Neurons, Oxygen & Nanak
The Education Decree
Principia Humanitas
The Krishna Cancer
Rowdy Buddha: The First Sapiens
We Are All Black: A Treatise on Racism
The Bengal Tigress: A Treatise on Gender Equality
Either Civilized or Phobic: A Treatise on Homosexuality
Wise Mating: A Treatise on Monogamy
Illusion of Religion: A Treatise on Religious
Fundamentalism
The Film Testament
Human Making is Our Mission: A Treatise on Parenting
I Am The Thread: My Mission
7 Billion Gods: Humans Above All
Lord is My Sheep: Gospel of Human
Morality Absolute
A Push in Perception
Let The Poor Be Your God
Conscience over Nonsense
Saint of The Sapiens
Time to Save Medicine
Fabric of Humanity

Build Bridges not Walls: In the name of Americana
The Constitution of The United Peoples of Earth
Lives to Serve Before I Sleep
When Humans Unite: Making A World Without Borders
All For Acceptance
Monk Meets World
Mission Reality
Citizens of Peace: Beyond The Savagery of Sovereignty
Operation Justice: To Make A Society That Needs No Law
See No Gender
The Gospel of Technology
Every Generation Needs Caretakers: The Gospel of
Patriotism
Aşkanjali: The Sufi Sermon
Mad About Humans: World Maker's Almanac
Revolution Indomable
When Call The People: My World My Responsibility
No Foreigner Only Family
Hurricane Humans: Give me accountability, I'll give you
peace
Ain't Enough to Look Human
Servitude is Sanctitude
Time To End Democracy: The Meritocratic Manifesto
I Vicdansaadet Speaking: No Rest Till The World is Lifted

DEDICATION

*This book is dedicated to my homeland,
the United States of America*

CONTENTS

1. We Are Born Animals

I was born an animal - you were born an animal - every human on earth is born an animal - none of us are actually born as humans. If you think the title human is your birthright, you couldn't be more wrong - it's not some family heirloom that is handed down through generations - each generation must earn the title human - and not just that, each generation must rediscover the very definition of the term human in their own way and make it evolve with the needs of the time. In short, the very definition of humanity must keep evolving with time, it mustn't stay rigid - for rigidity breeds disorder, evolution breeds fruitfulness.

How can we do that one wonders - and the answer is, through education. To instill and sustain justice and equality in the human society – or to put it simply, to instill, foster and further develop humanity in the human society, we need education, but not the kind of education we have been used to. Uneducated is not the one who doesn't have higher education, uneducated is the one who has no humanity in heart, despite having the highest of education that money can buy.

A child should be educated, not to earn a living, but to build a world. Any nation that puts this fundamental into action will advance beyond imagination. The purpose of education should be to make humans, not machines. Yet it is machines that today's education so proudly manufactures. Until this changes, society will continue to suffer from the lack of warmth, justice and humaneness. What is justice if not a common, everyday sense of community!

2. Seed of Justice

The seed of justice is education - a good education leads to a just society, a bad education leads to a savage society. An education that doesn't instill responsibility towards society, is nothing but a failure - and as such it is anything but education. Therefore, to make sure that education instills responsibility, we must humanize education first - and to do that we must humanize our very perception of education.

To reform society with education, we must reform education first. Reform education and you'd reform society. Education as we know today was devised ages ago to make mechanical slaves with no original thinking of their own, who are good at obeying commands. But we have left that savage society behind long ago, yet we continue to educate our children with the same kind of slave-producing education.

We may have added new subjects to the curriculum, but the method in which we teach those subjects remains the same. And if this kind of education continues then I'm afraid society will continue to suffer from disparity, injustice, bigotry and inhumanity.

Instead of teaching kids to memorize the answers to predetermined questions, we must inspire them to come up with their own questions. Show me a mediocre student with a lot of questions, I'll show you a genius - show me a smart student with a lot of answers, I'll show you second-hand human.

Education should be about learning to ask questions not memorizing answers, for today's answers won't solve tomorrow's problems. Tomorrow's problems will require new answers - and only those who can think for themselves, can come up with new answers, not those who are used to memorizing answers that already exist.

If you must memorize, then memorize this - one original question is more important than a hundred existing answers - one thought of wonder is more important than a hundred pages of facts - one act of curiosity is more important than a hundred degrees.

Curiosity is a thousand times more powerful than intelligence - intelligence can get you from A to B, but curiosity will get you through infinity. The world advances on the shoulders of curiosity, not intelligence. This is because intelligence works on preexisting data, whereas curiosity works not just on preexisting data, but more importantly on imagination and possibility.

3. Curiosity Kills Prejudice

At school I was a mediocre student, then at university I was a failed student, but today all of humankind have assimilated my ideas into their lives in the course of inclusion and harmony, and you know why - it is not because of my intelligence, but because of my curiosity.

Lack of curiosity is also the reason why prejudice continues to torture our society even in this day and age. When curiosity reigns, equality and justice are bound to flourish, for curiosity not only gives us understanding, but also keeps our biases in check - and when biases are in check prejudices wither and fade away.

Spare the biases, spoil the society. Biases are the lifeblood of prejudice - kill the biases and prejudices will die on their own. And when prejudices die, hate crimes come down exponentially.

No conviction is beyond scrutiny, for even the strongest of convictions may hold the most despicable of biases, which if left unchecked, can destroy an entire society. So question everything that you believe in, with the exception of your belief in yourself and in humanity. Scrutinize every single conviction that you hold dear -

make them pass through the gateway of reason before you let them get hold of your behavior.

When the people of a society care not for scrutinizing their convictions, nothing can stop the reign of injustice and discrimination - in such a society the privileged turn the fundamental of justice into a commodity. And when justice becomes a commodity in the marketplace of the court system, the citizens must take it upon themselves to conduct a complete overhaul of the very democracy they are living in.

And this transformation of democracy starts with the transformation of one's own psyche. It starts with standing up to one's own biases. And when the humans learn to stand up to their own biases, we'll no longer need any law to maintain order, for each human will be order incarnate themselves. Then any democracy such humans create will truly be a civilized one, contrary to what we have today.

4. Letter to Law Enforcement

Every field of human endeavor has its own unique problem. The problem with science is lack of warmth. The problem with philosophy is lack of empathy. The problem with religion is lack of reason. The problem with politics is lack of expertise. And the problem with law enforcement is not corruption, but an absolute denial of that corruption, and until you acknowledge that many of your officers are corrupt and prejudiced to the neck, you can never in a million years build a healthy relationship with the people.

Prejudices thrive on biases, and biases are a part of our psyche - of the human psyche, and no matter what we do, we cannot erase them from our mind - but we do have the ability to be aware of them, and only when we are aware of them, can we choose whether or not to be driven by them. However, when you don't even acknowledge that you have biases, that you are filled with prejudice, then you are inadvertently choosing not to accept the root of all the mistakes committed by you and your fellow officers in the line of duty.

A civilian may choose to stay biased and prejudiced all their life, but you as a defender of the people - as a defender of their rights, their security, their serenity - do not have the luxury to let your biases, to let your prejudices come in the way of your duty, for the moment they do, you the keeper of law and order, turn into the very cause of disorder.

Therefore, it's not enough for an officer of the law to have combat training and legal knowledge, it is also imperative that you learn about biases, that you learn about the fears, insecurities and instinctual tendencies of the human mind. An officer of the law without an understanding of biases, is like a ten year old with a knife - they may feel that they have power, but they have no clue as to the real life implications of that power. Remember my friend, power that doesn't help the people, is not power but pandemic.

Your combat training doesn't make you a police officer, for when enraged even an ordinary civilian can take down ten police officers - your knowledge of law doesn't make you an officer of the law, for when pushed even a mediocre college student can defeat an army of elite legal minds - what makes you a police officer is your absolute acceptance of your role in society - the role of selfless servants. Once you accept the role of selfless servants wholeheartedly, people are bound to trust you.

My brave, conscientious officers of the law, if you want people to trust you, don't use the phrase "police are your friends", for it only makes you sound authoritarian, egotistical and condescending - instead, remind them "police are humans too" - acknowledge your mistakes and work towards correcting them, so that you can truly become the Caretaker of People, which is the very definition of COP.

5. Police Sonnet

Police Sonnet

Police is not a profession,
But a promise of protection.
So long as you carry the badge,
You must discard self-preservation.
The thin blue line of service,
Is not for self-serving narcissists.
When your sole concern is society,
Only then can you uphold justice.
You mustn't become manikins of politics,
Nor of bureaucratic brutality.
Your allegiance is only to the people,
Their welfare will rescue your humanity.
In the sea of selfishness be the selfless drop,
Taking care of people you become a real cop.

6. When Biases Are in Power

Biases are the seeds of corruption, so to eliminate corruption from society we have to start by working on the biases. But here the first thing that I must mention is, we cannot eliminate biases from the human mind - a mind without biases is a fictitious mind - no matter how much we think that we are free from biases, we are not.

What we can do is question our convictions, so that we are aware of those biases, and when we are actually aware of our biases as biases, instead of being driven by them unknowingly, we can choose not to act upon them. Now the question is why - because that's the only act different from the animals. The survival of an animal is predicated on how swiftly it can act on its primitive biases, in other words instincts, whereas the integrity of the fabric of human society is predicated on how conscientiously you can restrain your biases.

Biases will continue to drag us down to the level of animals - but you do have the brain capacity to not let them - nourish your conscience with all your might and let it guide your convictions, your emotions, your actions. When your biases are in control, you are a selfish animal, but when your conscience is in control, you are an actual human being.

When your biases are in power, all petty labels seem important, but once you get hold of your biases and place conscience in power, you start to see what's really important, that is, humanity. However, if your conscience is malnourished then it is very likely that even your conscience will act in favor of your biases, that is, in favor of your beliefs.

Let me give you an example, the conscience of the current administration (during 2020 that is) in the White House is so malnourished that it fails to recognize the irreversible trauma it has caused on hundreds of kids in the name of law and order. They are driven by their savage biases to such an extreme that they are absolutely incapable of realizing how it feels for a child to be separated from their parents. And in a society where this happens in the name of law, is anything but civilized.

Better have an immigrant without papers, than a child without parents. The kids separated from their parents suffer the same trauma as that of the victims of human trafficking, therefore the administration that conducts such savagery in the name of immigration law must face the same legal consequence as human traffickers do, and if law fails to hold them accountable, the people must do it.

Remember, nothing is above the people, not the president, not the law, not the court, not even the constitution - all these are there to serve the people, and when they stop serving all the people, and start serving only the rich and privileged, they inadvertently sign their death warrant, hence then it's time for the people to rise from the ashes of innocence as the fire of justice dismantling all that's rigid, corrupt and disfigured and rebuild a new society - a society for the humans, by the humans, of the humans.

7. Citizen Justice
(A Sonnet)

Citizen Justice
(A Sonnet)

Boldly comes justice,
Not just in color blue.
Boldly comes justice,
To make this world anew.
Boldly comes justice,
To defend the fellow innocent.
Boldly comes justice,
Upright, rational and fervent.
Boldly comes justice,
Crossing race, religion and gender.
Boldly comes justice,
To confront humanity's offender.
Justice on earth is no legal matter,
If one soul is hurt all must rise together.

.

34

8. Fundamentals of Justice

Some may argue, how can the people in a civilized society take law into their hands - to them I say, there is a difference between taking law into your own hands and revolution against injustice - and moreover, a society where the government is filled with self-serving egomaniacs and where the court system stands mute as a dumb spectator, is anything but a civilized society - it is a savage society, and the first step to transform it into a civilized one is to overthrow those corrupt authorities by any means necessary (homicide and torture aside). Remember, justice isn't sold by the dozen at Target, justice must be produced out of our own blood and sweat. So, be ready to bleed in the eternal struggle against injustice, or else our children may never know the true meaning of justice.

But again, please - please - please be very careful where injustice is concerned. It's imperative that our struggle for justice is guided by conscience and not vengeance. The moment we let our vengeance drive our revolution, is the moment we become the very oppressor we are fighting against.

Remember, nothing is black and white in our world and it never will be, so you must act out of accountability, not out of sheer aggression. Never forget why you are fighting the battle you are fighting, for once you forget your motive, there'll no longer be any difference between you and a common criminal.

For example, if the black people start treating all white people the way they have been treated by white supremacists, then there would no longer be any difference between them and the racists - in fact, they would become the new racists - if women start treating men the way they have been treat by misogynists, then there would no longer be any difference between them and the misogynists.

Black doesn't mean dangerous, white doesn't mean trash, brown doesn't mean smuggler, muslim doesn't mean terrorist, woman doesn't mean weak, and lgbt doesn't mean sick. These are the fundamentals that we must realize if we are to build a just and humane society.

Mark you, I mentioned that we are to build a just and humane society, not the government, not the state, for they are incapable of doing so.

Human society is in human hands, not in the hands of meritless authorities – not in the hands of characterless bigots – not in the hands of spineless opportunists.

9. Monarchy Sonnet

42

Monarchy Sonnet

Bloodline doesn't determine destiny,
Only determination can do that.
Biology doesn't see royalty,
Only bugs without backbone do that.
They say above the law is nobody,
Yet the royalty makes their own law.
If this is what civilization is about,
It's much better to be an outlaw.
The very existence of monarchy,
Is a sign of a medieval society.
We deny visa to hopes and ambition,
Yet kings and queens receive undeniable loyalty.
So I address the monarchs of planet earth,
Grow up and give your character a real birth.

10. The American Sonnet

46

The American Sonnet

On Mayflower we arrived filled with hope,
Escaping persecution and atrocities.
Upon landing we became the persecutor,
And atrociously evicted communities.
Apparently we were civilized people,
Who wanted it all for ourselves.
We snatched it all from the innocent natives,
And gave reservations to help themselves.
Even today we ignore these atrocities,
And continue to perpetuate segregation.
We may look civilized on the outside,
Inside we are walking discrimination.
We are the land of liberty but only in theory,
It's time to walk the talk and embody the glory.

11. The Presidential Sonnet

The Presidential Sonnet

This little sonnet I give to thee,
Who is to lead our land of the free.
Rising above all personal glee,
Open your eyes to what others can't see.
The path you seek your heart will pave,
For you to protect our home of the brave.
In case you fall into the corruption grave,
Awaken your dignity and do not rave.
I write this sonnet in ink of humanity,
So that you never forget your priority.
Stand upright and never you accept pity,
For you are to lead our land of liberty.
Let's sail boldly into the storms of annihilation,
Breathing light into dark by sheer determination.

52

12. Law and Disorder

So long as the world is run by meritless and backboneless governments and glass house lawmakers, we will not be able to transform it into a civilized, just and humane society, free from disparities, free from assaults, free from all sorts of inhumanities, for governments feed on the insecurities of the people.

Let me elaborate with an example. Governments cannot ensure the safety of women, law enforcement cannot ensure the safety of women, the only people who can are the women themselves, so destroy all expectations from law, policies and politics my brave sisters, and become your own defense - learn about the human anatomy, make martial arts a part of your life and teach your daughters the same, for I am ashamed to say this but I must, we are yet to become a civilized society - so if and when the unfortunate moment arrives that some misogynist buffoon makes a pass without consent, you will be able to not only defend your own dignity, but also teach him a lesson never to forget - the lesson of not just respect, but civilized human behavior.

After the wrong has been done, sending the animals to cages does not prevent others from committing animal behavior - to prevent that they must know in their bones that one wrong move and their very life will be in danger. And this cannot happen by the intervention of law, for if it could, the barbarian issues of harassment and assault would've disappeared from earth long ago.

When the wrong is done, no policy and no law can undo it, so you must be able to stop that wrong from happening in the first place. And to do that you must become self-reliant. I am not talking about you taking law into your hands, but you must take justice into your hands, for justice is born of the people, law may try codify it and imprison it in books in the pursuit of ensuring order, and that may work in certain aspects of society, but not all, and here we are talking about such an aspect where it doesn't work.

The terms law and order are used together and exactly in that order to keep people subconsciously convinced that order can be ensured only by law, whereas in a civilized society, the phrase should be "accountability and order" - that is, in a civilized society order is ensured only by accountability.

Law doesn't prevent disorder, it only punishes disorder with the fairytale hope that it would somehow prevent further disorder, and it may seem sound theoretically, but in real life it doesn't work. If it did, there wouldn't be any crime in the world.

Hence the phrase that we should practice as gospel is "accountability and order" - without the accountability of the ordinary, everyday individual humans, order can never reign in our society. Be accountable for your neighborhood - be accountable for your society - be accountable for the world. The world is not under the care of lawmakers and lawkeepers - our world must be taken care of by each one of us, no matter who we are, no matter what we do.

13. The Voting Sonnet

The Voting Sonnet

Why should you vote you ask,
Since it changes nothing!
And nothing will change,
By acting the indifferent weakling.
If you want things to change,
Support character not charisma.
Trash all your populist snobbery,
And it'll abolish all political miasma.
Politics is manipulation,
But it is so due to your gullibility.
Seek out the leader with backbone,
Only then there'll be hope for humanity.
But if you find not a leader of character,
Arise and be the one you seek here and there.

62

14. Two Liberties
(A Sonnet)

Two Liberties
(A Sonnet)

There is not one but two liberties,
One is savage and the other is civilized.
Savage liberty lacks accountability,
The civilized one makes us humanized.
In the jungle liberty is the supreme law,
But one that involves no accountability.
Thus injustice is the norm of wildlife,
But it can't be accepted in human society.
Accountability is the line of control,
Between human and animal behavior.
You don't need intellect to draw the line,
All you need is a well-formed character.
So liberty must be guided by accountability,
Only then can we create a sane society.

15. When Liberty and Injustice Walk Together

Nobody can give liberty to nobody, for liberty is intrinsic to every life on earth. However the mental and physiological maturity of the life determines whether the practice of liberty of one lifeform will compromise the liberty of another lifeform. For example, though there are various aspects in which we can reduce the slaughter and torture of animal life, we'll still need to carry out such atrocity in some aspects to ensure the health and wellbeing of human society, such as in clinical trials for pills and treatments and in food production.

However, as we continue to advance in science and technology, we will one day no longer need to harm animals for human welfare - one day practice of human liberty will not come at the cost of animal liberty. But right now we are not yet advanced enough to ensure human welfare without harming animals. So for now, while talking about liberty, we are talking specifically about human liberty in human society.

Liberty and justice are intertwined with each other. Let me elaborate. By practicing our liberty we are being unjust to the animals. And harsh and immoral though it may sound, this is something we cannot prevent, but what about being unjust to other humans by practicing our liberty - that my friend, is completely preventable, and in fact, only when we prevent such unjust behavior, can we call ourselves human.

Absolute liberty makes a jungle out of our society, it's only with liberty guided by accountability that we can build a civilized society. In the absence of accountability, liberty and injustice go hand in hand, but where the people are accountable, no injustice can be born from the practice of their liberty.

In short, it's with accountability that we ought to lay the foundation of society, not with the unrestrained pursuit of liberty, for as far as life on earth is concerned, liberty has always been unrestrained to begin with. Doing whatever we feel like doing is nothing new or civilized, every animal on earth has been doing so since time immemorial - what's really civilized is to take into consideration the implication of our liberty on the lives of others.

Once we learn to meditate on the implications of our actions in our society, only then we will have the right to raise our head with conscience.

And that's the kind of meditation that the world is in desperate need of. The world doesn't need more meditation on slogans and mantras and imaginary entities - what the world needs is meditation on justice - it needs meditation on equality - it needs meditation on inclusion. Only with such meditation can we make sure that serenity, sanity and sanctity pervade inside of us and all around us. Or else our unrestraint pursuit of liberty will continue to keep us from building a true human civilization.

Remember, whether our shelters are made of concrete or tree branches, if we have no accountability in our heart towards the welfare of our society, we are just well-dressed animals. If independence is your right, then accountability is your duty - without accountability there is no difference between an independent human and an independent animal.

You can dress up a chimpanzee in a fancy suit, but that doesn't turn the chimpanzee into a human, but if that chimp can share his meal with another hungry chimp, then that chimp is more human than all of the selfish humanity combined. Appearance doesn't make you human, your behavior does - your accountability does - your sense of community does.

16. Why Governments Exist

74

Question everything, question your convictions - question your beliefs - question the convictions passed on to you by your culture - by your tradition - by your environment - by your government. Be informed, practice reason and act with conscience – that's the golden principle of a civilized society.

No government wants their citizens to be well informed, for when the citizens are well informed and start thinking for themselves, governments will have nothing to do, hence the very concept of government will disappear from the face of earth. The very existence of government or state is predicated upon the stupidity of the citizens - the more stupid the masses, the more powerful the government.

Hence, reason, truth, understanding all these are inconvenient to the politicians of our so-called democracy, for they can keep their power and position so long as they can keep you uninformed - because an uninformed citizenry is a docile citizenry - the more uninformed you are, the easier it is to control you.

You know why science works and democracy doesn't, it's because in science efficiency is the norm and inefficiency is unacceptable (that is inefficiency must be corrected), whereas in democracy inefficiency is the norm and efficiency is inconvenient. Here I am not saying that science is perfect - of course science has its flaws as well, but its good outweighs its bad – whereas when it comes to democracy people simply make it a habit to get used to all the bad while forgetting the fact that it is actually supposed to do good.

To put it simply, people have gotten used to the inefficiencies of those running democracy. So, to make our democracy actually work in favor of harmony, justice and progress, as opposed to segregation, bigotry and corruption, we the people must get rid of our savage indifference to inefficiencies - in short you must stop being the dumb spectator and start being an active builder of your society.

Feel for others, think for others, act for others - only then can you call yourself human. Remember, to build a society is no work of couch potatoes and closet philosophers - it's the work of living and breathing human beings, for anyone who doesn't feel responsible for the society is anything but human.

Justice pours out into the world from each footstep of alive human beings like lava from a volcano. And when an entire population turns cold and become the very definition of indifference in the face of injustice and corruption, a handful of humans must explode over the world like a volcano.

Arrogance and snobbery do not solve the society's problems, it needs actual rational solutions, and solutions are born only of care and concern, not of indifference and nonchalance. Do you care for the society, as much as you care for yourself or your immediate family?

It's not enough to live while you are alive, you must live even after you are dead, and to live even after death you must do good while you are alive. Life can't be measured by the breaths you take, but by the goodness you radiate in your everyday, ordinary behavior with others. Only with this ordinary, non-pompous, non-shallow, non-self-centric goodness can we instill peace and assimilation in our world. No goodness, no peace - no goodness, no assimilation – no goodness, no justice.

17. Sonnet of International Relations

Sonnet of International Relations

Modern dictators don't use oppression,
To keep thought and liberty barred.
The effective means of new dictatorship,
Is to play the nationalism card.
Feed people lies covered with nationalism,
They'll applaud you without a but.
Talk about reason and inclusion,
They'll ignore you as a universalist nut.
Till today society thrives on sectarianism,
While arguing over peace and harmony.
We call this insanity international relations,
In our every act we empower disparity.
Still if we don't discard this sectarian savagery,
General Assemblies will sustain agony not amity.

82

18. Gospel of World Peace

World peace is nonsense, because the world that we have built is one that favors conflict and segregation over peace and harmony. Therefore to actually make world peace a reality, we must first reform the world we are living in. We must reform it from a self-centric, narcissistic world into a society-centric, humble world. And this reformation starts with ourselves, then from us it passes onto the children and from them to their children and so on.

Peace doesn't happen overnight, but if you do not reform yourself first, peace won't happen in a million years, no matter how many general assemblies you attend and no matter how many dialogues you have on how to have peace on earth.

The concept of world peace is nothing but a publicity stunt - for there to be real peace we actually have to stop living as tribal savages and start living as universal humans whose family are the humans, whose religion are the humans, whose philosophy are the humans.

It is this simple - peace starts with humans, not tribals. And so long as we continue to sustain the fabric of a tribal, that is, sectarian society, we will only have dialogues on peace, not peace itself. To make the dialogues on peace actually work, you must attend them with the genuine desire for the realization of peace instead of the desire for exclusive preservation of your own tribal identity.

If your own cultural identity is more important to you than unification of the world, then the world will remain segregated for the rest of time, but if you can truly, actually, genuinely aim towards the unification of the world even at the cost of your own identity, then not only we'll create a world of peace and assimilation, but also, in that world there will be place for all identities, with none of them being superior or inferior to any of them.

19. Knights of Naskar

88

You know who you are - you are the heroes of Naskar - you are the knights of Naskar - you have no relation with segregation - you have no attachment to bigotry - you have no allegiance to any ideology - the only allegiance that you have is not to me, not to any scripture, not to any school of thought, but to the humankind and humankind alone.

You are neither believers, nor nonbelievers, you are neither left, nor right, you are neither intellectual, nor ignorant, you are the whole human beings that the world so desperately needs - you are my order of new humans - humans beyond borders, humans beyond scriptures, humans beyond applause and mockery, beyond wealth and status, beyond anonymity and popularity.

You are the creator - you are the destroyer - so whine no more at the miseries of your life, for your life is not your own, it's the life that ought to be placed at the feet of others - at the feet of those who have no more hope - at the feet of those who are forgotten by the opportunist world created by a bunch of capitalist nincompoops.

For once open your eyes and look beyond your own pain, for the cure for your pain is held by the hearts of the destitute - rush to their rescue like a rainbearing cloud after a long period of drought and all your pains will get washed away by the torrents of joy born of your own two hands.

Do you feel out of breath - do you feel your throat drying up - do you feel your stomach crunching - that's exactly how I feel knowing that at this very moment there are countless lives across the world who have no roof over their head - who have no clothes on their back - who have no food on their plate - they don't even have the plate - knowing this I cannot sleep in peace a single day - so I do all that my mind and body are capable of to alleviate their suffering in the long run - don't waste your capacities on savage luxuries and stupid debates my friend - bring all your force out and be the hope to those living in hopelessness.

Joy is born in service, misery is born in selfishness. So whether you are going to be miserable or joyful is up to you. How you ask! Society teaches you to find joy in the benefit of the self, as a result everyone grows up to be miserable, for the more you seek joy for yourself the more joy runs away from you, but the moment you forget the self and walk down the path of service to benefit others, joy comes running after you.

To hell with your own pleasures, to hell with your own smiles, to hell with your own happiness, let go of all that pettiness and unleash the human into the world - unleash the human to seek out happiness for others - to seek out joy for others - to seek out the life that has gone lost from the existence of the innocent souls.

They have no messiah to resort to - and no messiah is going to appear from the sky to take away their miseries, for the only messiah that can do that is you - you who has a heart - you who has grace - you who is the very vessel of all-powerful sanctitude.

Your blood is not blood but a fountain of goodness - yet you waste it on selfish satisfactions - no more my friend, no more o brave maker of the world - make that river flow where it is most needed - let it rush to the rescue of those who are trampled by the luxuries of the

privileged - only then will you have the right to
be called human.

92

BIBLIOGRAPHY

Archer M., (2000), Being Human: The Problem of Agency. Cambridge University Press.

Archer M., (2003), Structure, Agency and the Internal Conversation. Cambridge University Press.

Adolphs R (2003) Cognitive neuroscience of human social behaviour. Nature Rev Neurosci 4: 165–178.

Adolphs R, Tranel D, Damasio AR (2003) Dissociable neural systems for recognizing emotions. Brain Cogn 52: 61–69.

Afton, A. D. (1985). Forced copulation as a reproductive strategy of male lesser scaup: A field test of some predictions. - Behaviour 92, p. 146-167.

Allison T, Puce A, McCarthy G. (2000) Social perception from visual cues: role of the STS region. Trends Cogn Sci 4: 267–278.

Andresen, Jensine, and Robert Forman, eds. Cognitive Models and Spiritual Maps. Bowling Green, Ohio: Imprint Academic, 2000.

Ashbrook, James, and Carol Albright. The Humanizing Brain: Where Religion and Neuroscience Meet. Cleveland, OH: Pilgrim Press, 1997.

Azari, Nina, Janpeter Nickel, Gilbert Wunderlich, Michael Niedeggen, Harald Hefter, Lutz Tellmann, Hans Herzog, Petra Stoerig, Dieter Birnbacher, and Rudiger Seitz. "Neural Correlates of Religious Experience." European Journal of Neuroscience 13, no. 8 (2001)

Agar, N. (2004). Liberal eugenics: In defence of human enhancement. London: Blackwell Publishing.

Alteheld, N., Roessler, G., Vobig, M., & Walter, R. (2004). The retina implant new approach to a visual prosthesis. Biomedizinische Technik, 49(4), 99–103.

Antal, A., Nitsche, M. A., Kincses, T. Z., Kruse, W., Hoffmann, K. P., & Paulus, W. (2004a). Facilitation of visuo-motor learning by transcranial direct current stimulation of the motor and extrastriate visual areas in humans. European Journal of Neuroscience, 19(10), 2888–2892.

Bhat Z, Kumar, S, Bhat H (2015) In vitro meat production. Challenges and benefits over conventional meat production. J Sci Food Agric 14: 241–248

Bernstein R. J., (1967), John Dewey. New York: Washington Square Press.

Bernstein R.J., (1971), Praxis and Action: Contemporary Philosophies of Human Activity. Philadelphia: University of Pennsylvania Press.

Bernstein R.J., (1976), The Restructuring Social and Political Thought.

Bernstein R.J., (1983), Beyond Relativism and Objectivism: Science, Hermeneutics, and Praxis. Philadelphia: University of Pennsylvania Press.

Bernstein R.J., (1986), Philosophical Profiles. Philadelphia: University of Pennsylvania Press.

Bernstein R.J., (1991), New Constellation. Cambridge: MIT Press.

Barash, D. P. (1977). Sociobiology of rape in mallards (Anas platyrhynchos): Responses of the mated male. - Science 197, p. 788-789.

Berger, J. (1986). Wild horses of the great basin: Social competition and population size. - The University of Chicago Press, Chicago.

Birkhead, T. R., Johnson, S. D. & Nettleship, D. N. (1985). Extra-pair matings and mate guarding in the common murre Uria aalge. - Anim. Behav. 33, p. 608-619.

Beauregard, Mario, and Vincent Paquette. "Neural Correlates of a Mystical Experience in Carmelite Nuns." Neuroscience Letters 405, no. 3 (2006)

Benson, Herbert. Timeless Healing: The Power and Biology of Belief. New York: Scribner, 1996

Bogen, J.E.(1995a), 'On the neurophysiology of consciousness: Part I. An overview', Consciousness and Cognition, 4.

Bogen, J.E. (1995b), 'On the neurophysiology of consciousness: Part II. Constraining the semantic problem', Consciousness and Cognition, 4.

Bremner, J. D., R. Soufer, et al. (2001). "Gender differences in cognitive and neural correlates of remembrance of emotional words." Psychopharmacol Bull 35 (3).

Brothers, L. (2002). The social brain: A project for integrating primate behavior and neurophysiology in a new domain. In J. T. Cacioppo et al. (Eds.), Foundations in neuroscience. Cambridge, MA: MIT Press.

Buss, D. D. (2003). Evolutionary Psychology: The New Science of Mind, 2nd ed. New York: Allyn & Bacon.

Buss, D. M. (1989). "Conflict between the sexes: Strategic interference and the evocation of anger and upset." J Pers Soc Psychol 56 (5).

Buss, D. M. (1995). "Psychological sex differences. Origins through sexual selection." Am Psychol 50 (3).

Buss, D. M. (2002). "Review: Human Mate Guarding." Neuro Endocrinol Lett 23 (Suppl 4).

Buss, D. M., and D. P. Schmitt (1993). "Sexual strategies theory: An evolutionary perspective on human mating." Psychol Rev 100 (2).

Blakemore SJ, Decety J (2001) From the perception of action to the understanding of intention. Nature Rev Neurosci 2: 561.

Bruce C, Desimone R, Gross CG (1981) Visual properties of neurons in a polysensory area in superior temporal sulcus of the macaque. J Neurophysiol 46: 369–384.

Buccino G, Vogt S, Ritzl A, Fink GR, Zilles K, Freund HJ, Rizzolatti G (2004) Neural circuits underlying imitation of hand actions: an event related fMRI study. Neuron 42: 323–34.

Colapietro V., (1988), "Human Agency: The Habits of Our Being."

Southern Journal of Philosophy, XXVI, 2, pp. 153-68.

Colapietro V., (1992), "Purpose, Power, and Agency." The Monist, 75, 4 (October) pp. 423-44.

Colapietro V., (2003), "Signs and their vicissitudes: Meanings in excess of consciousness and functionality." Logica, Dialogica, Ideologica, a cure di Susan Petrilli e Patrizia Calefato (Milano: Mimesis), pp. 221-36.

Colapietro V., (2004a), "C. S. Peirce's Reclamation of Teleology." Nature in American Philosophy, ed. Jean De Groot (Washington, D.C.: Catholic University Press of America), pp. 88-108.

Colapietro V., (2004b), "Portrait of a Historicist: An Alternative Reading of Peircean Semiotic." Semiotiche, 2/04 [maggio 2004], pp. 49-68.

Colapietro V., (2006), "Engaged Pluralism: Between Alterity and

Sociality." The Pragmatic Century: Conversations with Richard J. Bernstein (Albany, NY: SUNY Press), pp. 39-68.

Colapietro V., (2009), "Habit, Competence, and Purpose." Forthcoming in The Transactions of the Charles S. Peirce Society. Calder AJ, Keane J, Manes F, Antoun N, Young AW (2000) Impaired recognition and experience of disgust following brain injury. Nature Neurosci 3: 1077–1078.

Carey DP, Perrett DI, Oram MW (1997) Recognizing, understanding and reproducing actions. In: Jeannerod M, Grafman J (eds) Handbook of neuropsychology. Vol. 11: Action and cognition. Elsevier, Amsterdam.

Carr L, Iacoboni M, Dubeau MC, Mazziotta JC, Lenzi GL (2003) Neural mechanisms of empathy in humans: a relay from neural systems for imitation to limbic areas. Proc Natl Acad Sci USA 100: 5497–5502.

Changeux JP, Ricoeur P (1998) La nature et la règle. Odile Jacob, Paris.

Cochin S, Barthelemy C, Roux S, Martineau J (1999) Observation and execution of movement: similarities demonstrated by quantified electroencephalograpy. Eur J Neurosci 11: 1839– 1842.

Chomsky Noam, (2017) Requiem for the American Dream

Chomsky Noam, (2016) Who Rules the World?

Chomsky Noam, (2010) How the World Works

Churchland, P.S. (1986), Neurophilosophy (Cambridge, MA: The MIT Press).

Churchland, P.S. & Ramachandran, V.S. (1993), 'Filling in: Why Dennett is wrong', in Dennett and His Critics:

Demystifying Mind, ed. B. Dahlbom (Oxford: Blackwell Scientific Press).

Churchland, P.S., Ramachandran, V.S. & Sejnowski, T.J. (1994), 'A critique of pure vision', in Large- scale Neuronal Theories of the Brain, ed. C. Koch & J.L. Davis (Cambridge, MA: The MIT Press).

Crick, F. (1994), The Astonishing Hypothesis: The Scientific Search for the Soul (New York: Simon and Schuster).

Crick, F. (1996), 'Visual perception: rivalry and consciousness', Nature, 379.

Crick, F. & Koch, C. (1992), 'The problem of consciousness', Scientific American, 267.

Craig AD (2002) How do you feel? Interoception: the sense of the physiological condition of the body. Nature Rev Neurosci 3: 655–666.

Damasio, A (2003a) Looking for Spinoza. Harcourt Inc. Damasio A (2003b) Feeling of emotion and the self. Ann NY Acad Sci 1001: 253–261.

d'Aquili, Eugene. "Senses of Reality in Science and Religion." Zygon 17, no 4 (1982)

d'Aquili, Eugene. "The Biopsychological Determinants of Religious Ritual Behavior." Zygon 10, no. 1 (1975)

d'Aquili, Eugene. "The Myth-Ritual Complex: A Biogenetic Structural Analysis." Zygon 18, no. 3 (1983)

d'Aquili, Eugene, and Andrew Newberg. The Mystical Mind: Probing the Biology of Religious Experience. Minneapolis: Fortress Press, 1999.

Daly DD. 1958. Ictal affect. Am J Psychiatry.

Damasio, A. (1994) Descartes' Error: Emotion, Reason and the Human Brain. New York, Putnams.

Damasio, A. (1999) The Feeling of What Happens: Body, Emotion and the Making of Consciousness. London, Heinemann.

Darwin, C. (1859) On the Origin of Species by Means of Natural Selection. London, Murray.

Darwin, C. (1871) The Descent of Man and Selection in Relation to Sex. London, John Murray.

Darwin, C. (1872) The Expression of the Emotions in Man and Animals. London, John Murray; also published 1965, Chicago, University of Chicago Press.

Dawkins, M.S. (1987) Minding and mattering. In C. Blakemore and S. Greenfield (eds) Mindwaves. Oxford, Blackwell, 151-60.

Dawkins, R. (1976) The Selfish Gene. Oxford, Oxford University Press; a new edition, with additional material, was published in 1989.

Dawkins, R. (1986) The Blind Watchmaker. London, Longman.

Di Pellegrino G, Fadiga L, Fogassi L, Gallese V, Rizzolatti G (1992) Understanding motor events: A neurophysiological study. Exp Brain Res 91: 176–80.

Deikman, A.J. (2000) A functional approach to mysticism. Journal of Consciousness Studies 7(11-12), 75-91.

Delmonte, M.M. (1987) Personality and meditation. In M. West (ed.) The Psychology of Meditation. Oxford, Clarendon Press, 118-32.

Dennett, D.C. (1987) The Intentional Stance. Cambridge, MA, MIT Press.

Dennett, D.C. (1988) Quining qualia. In A.J. Marcel and E. Bisiach (eds)

Consciousness in Contemporary Science. Oxford, Oxford University Press, 42-77.

Dennett, D.C. (1991) Consciousness Explained. Boston, MA, and London, Little, Brown and Co.

Dennett, D.C. (1995a) Darwin's Dangerous Idea. London, Penguin.

Dennett, D.C. (1995b) The unimagined preposterousness of zombies. Journal of Consciousness Studies 2(4), 322-6.

Dennett, D.C. (1995c) Cog: steps towards consciousness in robots. In T. Metzinger (ed.) Conscious Experience. Thorverton, Devon, Imprint Academic, 471-87.

Dennett, D.C. (1995d) The path not taken. Behavioral and Brain Sciences 18, 252-3; commentary on N. Block, On a confusion about a function of consciousness. Behavioral and Brain Sciences 18, 227.

Dennett, D.C. (1996a) Facing backwards on the problem of consciousness. Journal of Consciousness Studies 3(1), 4-6.

Dennett, D.C. (1996b) Kinds of Minds: Towards an Understanding of Consciousness. London, Weidenfeld & Nicolson.

Dennett, D.C. (1997) An exchange with Daniel Dennett. In J. Searle (ed.) The Mystery of Consciousness. New York, New York Review of Books, 115-19.

Dennett, D.C. (1998) The myth of double transduction. In S.R. Hameroff, A.W. Kaszniak and A. C. Scott (eds) Toward a Science of Consciousness: The Second Tucson Discussions and Debates. Cambridge, MA, MIT Press, 97-107.

Dennett, D.C. (1998b) Brainchildren: Essays on Designing Minds. Cambridge, MA, MIT Press.

Dennett, D.C. (2001) The fantasy of first person science. Debate with D. Chalmers, Northwestern University, Evanston, IL, February 2001.

Dennett, D.C. (2003) Freedom Evolves. New York, Penguin.

Dennett, D.C. and Kinsbourne, M. (1992) Time and the observer: the where and when of consciousness in the brain. Behavioral and Brain Sciences 15, 183-247, including commentaries and authors' responses.

Dewey J., (1911 [1977]), "Epistemological Realism: The Alleged Ubiquity of the Knowledge Relation." Journal of Philosophy, VIII, 20 (September 28, 1911).

Dewhurst, Kenneth, and A. W. Beard. "Sudden Religious Conversions in Temporal Lobe Epilepsy." British Journal of Psychiatry 117 (1970)

Dewhurst K, Beard AW. Sudden religious conversions in temporal lobe epilepsy. 1970 Epilepsy Behav 2003

Devinsky O, Lai G. Spirituality and religion in epilepsy. Epilepsy Behav 2008.

Devinsky, O., Morrell, MJ, Vogt, BA. (1995) 'Contribution of anterior cingulate cortex to behavior', Brain, 118.

Douglas Stone A., Chapter 24, The Indian Comet, in the book Einstein and the Quantum, Princeton University Press, Princeton, New Jersey, 2013.

E. Horvitz, "One Hundred Year Study on Artificial Intelligence: Reflections and Framing," ed: Stanford University, 2014.

Einstein A. (1925). "Quantentheorie des einatomigen idealen Gases". Sitzungsberichte der Preussischen Akademie der Wissenschaften.

Eckhart Meister, Selected Writings

Egidi R., ed. (1999), "Von Wright and 'Dante's Dream': Stages in a Philosophical Pilgrim's Progress", in In Search of a New Humanism: the Philosophy of G.H. von Wright, ed. by R. Egidi, Kluwer, Dordrecht.

Fadiga L, Fogassi L, Pavesi G, Rizzolatti G (1995) Motor facilitation during action observation: a magnetic stimulation study. J Neurophysiol 73: 2608–2611.

Fogassi L, Gallese V, Fadiga L, Rizzolatti G (1998) Neurons responding to the sight of goal directed hand/arm actions in the parietal area PF (7b) of the macaque monkey. Soc Neurosci Abs 24:257.5.

Frith U, Frith CD (2003) Development and neurophysiology of mentalizing. Philos Trans R Soc Lond B Biol Sci 358: 459.

Farah, M.J. (1989), 'The neural basis of mental imagery', Trends in Neurosciences, 10.

Finlay BL, Darlington RB (1995) Linked regularities in the development and evolution of mammalian brains. Science 268.

Freud, S. "The Interpretation of Dreams", 1900

Freud, S. "Selected papers on hysteria and other psychoneuroses" Journal of Nervous and Mental Disease 1909.

Freud, S. "The Origin and Development of Psychoanalysis", 1910

Freud, S. "Psychopathology of everyday life", 1914

Freud, S. "Beyond the Pleasure Principle", 1920

Frith, C.D. & Dolan, R.J. (1997), 'Abnormal beliefs: Delusions and memory', Paper presented at the May,

1997, Harvard Conference on Memory and Belief.

Gay, Volney, ed. Neuroscience and Religion. Plymouth, UK: Lexington Books, 2009.

Gazzaniga, M. S. (1985). The social brain. New York: Basic Books.

Gazzaniga, M.S. (1993), 'Brain mechanisms and conscious experience', Ciba Foundation Symposium, 174.

Geschwind N. "Behavioural changes in temporal lobe epilepsy". Psychol Med. 1979.

Gellhorn, E., Kiely, W.F. "Mystical states of consciousness: neurophysiological and clinical aspects." J Nerv Ment Dis. 1972;154:399-405.

Gilbert SL, Dobyns WB, Lahn BT (2005) Genetic links between brain development and brain evolution. Nat Rev Genet 6.

Gray JA. The Psychology of Fear and Stress. 2nd ed. New York, NY: Cambridge University Press; 1988.

Gloor, P. (1992), 'Amygdala and temporal lobe epilepsy', in The Amygdala: Neurobiological Aspects of Emotion, Memory and Mental Dysfunction, ed J.P. Aggleton (New York: Wiley-Liss).

Greenspan, S. I. and S. G. Shanker (2004). The first idea: How symbols, language, and intelligence evolved from our early primate ancestors to modern humans. Cambridge, MA: Da Capo Press.

Grady, D. (1993), 'The vision thing: Mainly in the brain', Discover, June.

Gallagher HL, Frith CD (2003) Functional imaging of 'theory of mind'. Trends Cogn Sci 7: 77.

Gallese V, Fogassi L, Fadiga L, Rizzolatti G (2002) Action representation and the inferior parietal lobule. In: Prinz W, Hommel B (eds) Attention & Performance XIX. Common mechanisms in perception and action. Oxford University Press, Oxford.

Gallese V, Keysers C, Rizzolatti G (2004) A unifying view of the basis of social cognition. Trends Cogn Sci 8: 396–403.

Gangitano M, Mottaghy FM, Pascual-Leone A (2001) Phase specific modulation of cortical motor output during movement observation. NeuroReport 12: 1489–1492.

Gangitano M, Mottaghy FM, Pascual-Leone A (2004) Modulation of premotor mirror neuron activity during observation of unpredictable grasping movements. Eur J Neurosci 20: 2193– 2202.

Goldman AI, Sripada CS (2004) Simulationist models of face-based emotion recognition. Cognition 94: 193–213.

Grèzes J, Costes N, Decety J (1998) Top-down effect of strategy on the perception of human biological motion: a PET investigation. Cogn Neuropsychol 15: 553–582.

Grèzes J, Armony JL, Rowe J, Passingham RE (2003) Activations related to "mirror" and "canonical" neurones in the human brain: an fMRI study. Neuroimage 18: 928–937.

Gross CG, Rocha-Miranda CE, Bender DB (1972) Visual properties of neurons in the inferotemporal cortex of the macaque. J Neurophysiol 35: 96–111.

Hari R, Forss N, Avikainen S, Kirveskari S, Salenius S, Rizzolatti G (1998) Activation of human primary motor cortex during action observation: a neuromagnetic study.

Proc. Natl Acad Sci USA 95: 15061–15065.

Hardy, G. H. (1940). Ramanujan. Cambridge: Cambridge University Press.

Hall, Daniel, Keith Meador, and Harold Koenig. "Measuring Religiousness in Health Research: Review and Critique." Journal of Religion and Health 47, no. 2 (2008)

Harris, Sam, Jonas Kaplan, Ashley Curiel, Susan Bookheimer, Marco Iacoboni, and Mark Cohen. "The Neural Correlates of Religious and Nonreligious Belief." PLoS One 4, no. 10 (October 1, 2009)

Halgren, E. (1992), 'Emotional neurophysiology of the amygdala within the context of human cognition', in The Amygdala: Neurobiological Aspects of Emotion, Memory and Mental Dysfunction, ed J.P. Aggleton (New York: Wiley-Liss).

Halligan PW, Fink GR, Marshal JC, Vallar G. 2003. Spatial cognition: evidence from visual neglect. Trends Cogn Sci.

Handbook of Emotions, Edited by Michael Lewis, Jeannette M. Haviland-Jones, and Lisa Feldman Barrett, The Guilford Press; 3rd edition (2010).

Haggard, P., Clark, S. and Kalogeras,]. (2002) Voluntary action and conscious awareness, Nature Neuroscience 5, 382-5. Haggard, P., Newman, C. and Magno, E. (1999) On the perceived time of voluntary actions. British Journal of Psychology 90, 291-303.

Hameroff, S.R. and Penrose, R. (1996) Conscious events as orchestrated space-time selections. Journal of Consciousness Studies 3(1), 36-53; also reprinted in J. Shear (ed.) (1997) Explaining Consciousness-The Hard Problem. Cambridge, MA, MIT Press, 177-95.

Hardcastle, V.G. (2000) How to understand theN in NCC. InT. Metzinger (ed.) Neural Correlates of Consciousness. Cambridge, MA, MIT Press, 259-64.

Harding, D.E. (1961) On Having no Head: Zen and the Re-Discovery of the Obvious. London, Buddhist Society.

Hardy, A. (1979) The Spiritual Nature of Man: A Study of Contemporary Religious Experience. Oxford, Clarendon Press.

Hamad, S. (1990) The symbol grounding problem. Physica D 42, 335-46.

Hamad, S. (2001) No easy way out. The Sciences 41(2), 36-42.

Harre, R. and Gillett, G. (1994) The Discursive Mind. Thousand Oaks, CA, Sage.

Haugeland, J. (ed.) (1997) Mind Design II: Philosophy, Psychology, Artificial

Intelligence. Cambridge, MA, MIT Press.

Hauser, M.D. (2000) Wild Minds: What Animals Really Think. New York, Henry Holt and Co.; London, Penguin.

Hearne, K. (1990) The Dream Machine. Northants, Aquarian.

Hebb, D.O. (1949) The Organization of Behavior. New York, Wiley.

Helmholtz, H.L.F. von (1856-67) Treatise on Physiological Optics.

Hess, EH (1975) "The role of pupil size in communication," Scientific American, 233(5), 110–12.

Heyes, C.M. (1998) Theory of mind in nonhuman primates. Behavioral and Brain Sciences 21, 101-48; with commentaries.

Heyes, C.M. and Galef, B.G. (eds) (1996) Social Learning in Animals: The Roots of Culture. San Diego, CA, Academic Press.

Hilgard, E.R. (1986) Divided Consciousness: Multiple Controls in Human Thought and Action. New York, Wiley.

Hocquette JF (2016) Is in vitro meat the

solution for the future? Meat Science 120:

167–176

Hodgson, R. (1891) A case of double consciousness. Proceedings of the Society for Psychical Research 7, 221-58.

Hofstadter, D.R. (1979) Code!, Escher, Bach: An Eternal Golden Braid. London, Penguin.

Hofstadter, D.R. and Dennett, D.C. (eds) (1981) The Mind's I: Fantasies and Reflections on Self and Soul. London, Penguin.

Holland, J. (ed.) (2001) Ecstasy: The Complete Guide: A Comprehensive Look at the Risks and Benefits of

MDMA. Rochester, VT, Park Street Press.

Holmes, D.S. (1987) The influence of meditation versus rest on physiological arousal. In M. West (ed.) The Psychology of Meditation. Oxford, Clarendon Press, 81-103.

Holt, J. (1999) Blindsight in debates about qualia. Journal of Consciousness Studies 6(5), 54-71.

Horgan, J. (1994), 'Can science explain consciousness?', Scientific American, 271.

Holloway RL (1996) Evolution of the human brain. In: Lock A, Peters CR (eds) Handbook of human symbolic evolution. Oxford University Press, Oxford

Iacoboni M, Woods RP, Brass M, Bekkering H, Mazziotta JC, Rizzolatti G (1999) Cortical mechanisms of human imitation. Science 286: 2526-2528.

Iacoboni M, Koski LM, Brass M, Bekkering H, Woods RP, Dubeau MC, Mazziotta JC, Rizzolatti G (2001) Reafferent copies of imitated actions in the right superior temporal cortex. Proc Natl Acad Sci USA 98: 13995–13999.

Jeannerod M (1988) The neural and behavioural organization of goal-directed movements. Clarendon Press, Oxford.

Johnson-Frey SH, Maloof FR, Newman-Norlund R, Farrer C, Inati S, Grafton ST (2003) Actions or hand-objects interactions? Human inferior frontal cortex and action observation. Neuron 39: 1053–1058.

Jackson, F. (1982) Epiphenomenal qualia. Philosophical Quarterly 32, 127-36.

James, W. (1890) The Principles of Psychology (2 volumes). London, Macmillan.

James, W. (1902) The Varieties of Religious Experience: A Study in Human Nature. New York and London, Longmans, Green and Co.

Jansen, K. (2001) Ketamine: Dreams and Realities. Sarasota, FL, Multidisciplinary Association for Psychedelic Studies.

Jay, M. (ed.) (1999) Artificial Paradises: A Drugs Reader. London, Penguin.

Jaynes, J. (1976) The Origin of Consciousness in the Breakdown of the Bicameral Mind. New York, Houghton Mifflin.

Johnson, M.K. and Raye, C.L. (1981) Reality monitoring. Psychological Review 88, 67-85.

Kadim I, Mahgoub O, Baqir S et al. (2015) Cultured meat from muscle stem cells: a review of challenges and prospects. J Integr Agr 14: 222–233

Koski L, Iacoboni M, Dubeau MC, Woods RP, Mazziotta JC (2003) Modulation of cortical activity during different imitative behaviors. J Neurophysiol 89: 460–471.

Krolak-Salmon P, Henaff MA, Isnard J, Tallon-Baudry C, Guenot M, Vighetto A, Bertrand O, Mauguiere F (2003) An attention modulated response to disgust in human ventral anterior insula. Ann Neurol 53: 446–453.

Kandel, E. R. In Search of Memory: The Emergence of a New Science of Mind, W. W. Norton & Company (2007).

Kandel E. R. Schwartz JH, Jessel TM. Principles of neural sciences. New York; McGraw Hill, 2000.

Kanizsa, G. (1979), Organization In Vision (New York: Praeger).

Kaloupek DG, Scott JR, Khatami V. Assessment of coping strategies associated with syncope in blood donors. J Psychosom Res. 1985;29:207-214.

Kanwisher, N. (2001) Neural events and perceptual awareness. Cognition 79, 89-113; also reprinted inS. Dehaene (ed.) The Cognitive Neuroscience of Consciousness. Cambridge, MA, MIT Press, 89-113.

Kapleau, Roshi P. (1980) The Three Pillars of Zen: Teaching, Practice, and Enlightenment (revised edn). New York, Doubleday.

Karn, K. and Hayhoe, M. (2000) Memory representations guide targeting eye movements in a natural task. Visual Cognition 7, 673-703.

Kasamatsu, A. and Hirai, T. (1966) An electroencephalographic study on the Zen meditation (zazen). Folia Psychiatrica et Neurologica Japonica 20, 315-36.

Kaiserman-Abramof, I. R., Graybiel, A. M., & Nauta, W. J. (1980). The thalamic projection to cortical area 17 in a congenitally anophthalmic mouse strain. Neuroscience, 5, 41–52.

Kanold, P. O., Kara, P., Reid, R. C., & Shatz, C. J. (2003). Role of subplate neurons in functional maturation of visual cortical columns. Science, 301, 521–525.

Kennedy, H., & Dehay, C. (1988). Functional implications of the anatomical organization of the callosal projections of visual areas V1 and V2 in the macaque monkey. Behav. Brain Res., 29, 225–236.

Kentridge, R.W. and Heywood, C.A. (1999) The status of blindsight. Journal of Consciousness Studies 6(5), 3-11.

Kihlstrom, J.F. (1996) Perception without awareness of what is perceived, learning without awareness of what is learned. In M. Velmans (ed.) The Science of Consciousness. London, Routledge, 23-46.

Kollerstrom, N. (1999) The path of Halley's comet, and Newton's late apprehension of the law of gravity. Annals of Science 56, 331-56.

Kosslyn, S.M. (1980) Image and Mind. Cambridge, MA, Harvard University Press.

Kosslyn, S.M. (1988) Aspects of a cognitive neuroscience of mental imagery. Science 240, 1621-6.

Kinsbourne, M. (1995), 'The intralaminar thalamic nucleii', Consciousness and Cognition, 4.

Kjaer, Troels, Camilla Bertelsen, Paola Piccini, David Brooks, Jorgen Alving, and Hans Lou. "Increased Dopamine Tone during Meditation- Induced Change of Consciousness." Cognitive Brain Research 13, no. 2 (April 2002)

Kölmel HW. 1985. Complex visual hallucinations in the hemianopic field. J Neurol Neurosurg Psychiatry.

Koenig, Harold. "Research on Religion, Spirituality, and Mental Health: A Review." Canadian Journal of Psychiatry 54, no. 5 (May 2009)

Koenig, Harold, ed. Handbook of Religion and Mental Health. San Diego, CA: Academic Press, 1998

Kraepelin E. Psychiatry: A Textbook for Students and Physicians. New York, NY: Science History Publications; 1990.

Lauglin, Charles, John McManus, and Eugene d'Aquili. Brain, Symbol, and Experience. 2nd ed. New York: Columbia University Press, 1992

Lakoff, G. and M. Johnson (1999). Philosophy in the flesh. Basic Books: New York.

LeDoux, J. E. (1996). The emotional brain. New York: Simon & Schuster.

LeDoux, J.E. (1992), 'Emotion and the amygdala', in The Amygdala:

Neurobiological Aspects of Emo- tion, Memory and Mental Dysfunction, ed J.P. Aggleton (New York: Wiley-Liss).

Levin, D.T. and Simons, D.J. (1997) Failure to detect changes to attended objects in motion pictures. Psychonomic Bulletin and Review 4, 501-6.

Levine,J. (1983) Materialism and qualia: the explanatory gap. Pacific Philosophical Quarterly 64, 354-61.

Levine,J. (2001) Purple Haze: The Puzzle of Consciousness. New York, Oxford University Press. Levine, S. (1979) A Gradual Awakening. New York, Doubleday.

Levinson, B.W. (1965) States of awareness during general anaesthesia. British Journal of Anaesthesia 37, 544-6.

Lewicki, P., Czyzewska, M. and Hoffman, H. (1987) Unconscious acquisition of complex procedural knowledge. Journal of Experimental Psychology: Learning, Memory and Cognition 13, 523-30.

Lewicki, P., Hill, T. and Bizot, E. (1988) Acquisition of procedural knowledge about a pattern of stimuli that cannot be articulated. Cognitive Psychology 20, 24-37.

Lewicki, P., Hill, T. and Czyzewska, M. (1992) Nonconscious acquisition of information. American Psychologist 47, 796-801.

Manthey S, Schubotz RI, von Cramon DY (2003). Premotor cortex in observing erroneous action: an fMRI study. Brain Res Cogn Brain Res 15: 296–307.

Mesulam MM, Mufson EJ (1982) Insula of the old world monkey. III: Efferent cortical output and comments on function. J Comp Neurol 212: 38–52.

Naskar, Abhijit. "Homo: A Brief History of Consciousness", 2015

Naskar, Abhijit. "What is Mind?", 2016

Naskar, Abhijit. "Love, God & Neurons: Memoir of A Scientist who found himself by getting lost", 2016

Naskar, Abhijit. "Principia Humanitas", 2017

Naskar, Abhijit. "We Are All Black: A Treatise on Racism", 2017

Naskar, Abhijit. "Either Civilized or Phobic: A Treatise on Homosexuality", 2017

Naskar, Abhijit. "I Am The Thread: My Mission", 2017

Naskar, Abhijit. "The Bengal Tigress: A Treatise on Gender Equality", 2017

Naskar, Abhijit. "Morality Absolute", 2017

Naskar, Abhijit. "Build Bridges not Walls: In the name of Americana", 2018

Naskar, Abhijit. "Fabric of Humanity", 2018

Naskar, Abhijit. "Lives To Serve Before I Sleep", 2019

Naskar, Abhijit. "Citizens of Peace: Beyond the Savagery of Sovereignty", 2019

Naskar, Abhijit. "The Constitution of The United Peoples of Earth", 2019

Naskar, Abhijit. "Neurons Giveth, Neurons Taketh Away | Abhijit Naskar | TEDxIIMRanchi", 2019 https://www.youtube.com/watch?v=BNX-Q0ySm80

Naskar, Abhijit. "Mission Reality", 2019

Naskar, Abhijit. "Operation Justice: To Make A Society That Needs No Law", 2019

Naskar, Abhijit. "Every Generation Needs Caretakers: The Gospel of Patriotism", 2020

Naskar, Abhijit. "Revolution Indomable", 2020

Naskar, Abhijit. "Servitude is Sanctitude", 2020

Newberg, Andrew, and Jeremy Iversen. "The Neural Basis of the Complex Mental Task of Meditation: Neurotransmitter and Neurochemical Considerations." Medical Hypotheses 61, no. 2 (2003).

Newberg, Andrew. "How God Changes Your Brain: An Introduction to Jewish Neurotheology", CCAR Journal: The Reform Jewish Quarterly, Winter 2016.

Newberg, Andrew, and Stephanie Newberg. "A Neuropsychological Perspective on Spiritual Development." In Handbook of Spiritual Development in Childhood and Adolescence, edited by Eugene Roehlkepartain, Pamela King, Linda

Wagener, and Peter Benson. London: Sage Publications, Inc., 2005

Newberg, Andrew. "The Neurotheology Link An Intersection Between Spirituality and Health", Alternative and Complimentary Therapies, Vol 21 No 1, February 2015.

Newberg, Andrew, Nancy Wintering, Dharma Khalsa, Hannah Roggenkamp, and Mark Waldman. "Meditation Effects on Cognitive Function and Cerebral Blood Flow in Subjects with Memory Loss: A Preliminary Study." Journal of Alzheimer's Disease 20, no. 2 (2010)

Nash, M. (1995), 'Glimpses of the mind', Time.

Nesse RM. Proximate and evolutionary studies of anxiety, stress and depression: synergy at the interface. Neurosci Biobehav Rev. 1999;23:895-903.

Nicolelis, Miguel. (2011) "Beyond Boundaries: The New Neuroscience of Connecting Brains with Machines--- and How It Will Change Our Lives", Times Books

O'Hara, K. and Scutt, T. (1996) There is no hard problem of consciousness. Journal of Consciousness Studies 3(4), 290-302, reprinted in J. Shear (ed.) (1997) Explaining Consciousness. Cambridge, MA, MIT Press, 69-82.

O'Regan, J.K. (1992) Solving the "real" mysteries of visual perception: the world as an outside memory. Canadian Journal of Psychology 46, 461-88.

O'Regan, J.K. and Noe, A. (2001) A sensorimotor account of vision and visual consciousness. Behavioral and Brain Sciences 24(5), 883-917.

O'Regan, J.K., Rensink, R.A. and Clark,].]. (1999) Change-blindness as a result of "mudsplashes." Nature 398, 34.

Ornstein, R.E. (1977) The Psychology of Consciousness (2nd edn). New York, Harcourt.

Ornstein, R.E. (1986) The Psychology of Consciousness (3rd edn). New York, Pehguin.

Ornstein, R.E. (1992) The Evolution of Consciousness. New York, Touchstone.

Penfield W, Faulk ME (1955) The insula: further observations on its function. Brain 78: 445– 470.

Penrose, R. (1994), Shadows of the Mind (Oxford: Oxford University Press).

Penrose, R. (1989), The Emperor's New Mind: Concerning Computers, Minds and The Laws of Physics (Oxford: Oxford University Press).

Persinger, "'I would kill in God's name' role of sex, weekly church attendance, report of a religious experience and limbic lability" Perceptual and Motor Skills 1997.

Persinger "Experimental simulation of the God experience" Neurotheology 2003.

Persinger, M. A. (1993b). Personality changes following brain injury as a grief response to the loss of sense of self: Phenomenological themes as indices of local lability and neurocognitive restructuring as psycho- therapy. Psychological Reports, 72

Persinger, Corradini, Clement, Keaney, et al "Neurotheology and its convergence with neuroquantology" NeuroQuantology 2010.

Persinger, Koren and St-Pierre "The electromagnetic induction of mystical and altered states within the laboratory" Journal of Consciousness Exploration and Research 2010.

Persinger "Case report: A prototypical spontaneous 'sensed presence' of a sentient being and concomitant electroencephalographic activity in the clinical laboratory" Neurocase 2008.

Persinger and Saroka "Potential production of Hughlings Jackson's "parasitic consciousness" by physiologically-patterned weak transcerebral magnetic fields: QEEG and source localization" Epilepsy & Behavior 28 (2013).

Persinger. "The neuropsychiatry of paranormal experiences". J Neuropsychiatry Clin Neurosci 2001.

Persinger. "Neuropsychological bases of god beliefs", New York: Praeger, 1987

Persinger. "Temporal lobe epileptic signs and correlative behaviors displayed by normal populations", Journal of General Psychology, 1986

Perry BD, Pollard R. Homeostasis, stress, trauma, and adaptation. A neurodevelopmental view of childhood trauma. Child Adolesc Psychiatr Clin N Am. 1998;7:33.

Paré, D. & Llinás, R. (1995), 'Conscious and preconscious processes as seen from the standpoint of sleep-waking cycle neurophysiology', Neuropsychologia, 33.

P. S. de Laplace. Essai Philosophique sur les Probabilites [1814], in Academy des Sciences, Oeuvres Complotes de Laplace, Vol. 7, Gauthier-Villars, Paris (1886).

Perrett DI, Harries MH, Bevan R, Thomas S, Benson PJ, Mistlin AJ, Chitty AJ, Hietanen JK, Ortega JE (1989) Frameworks of analysis for the neural representation of animate objects and actions. J Exp Bio 146: 87–113.

Phillips ML, Young AW, Senior C, Brammer M, Andrew C, Calder AJ, Bullmore ET, Perrett DI, Rowland D, Williams SC, Gray JA, David AS (1997) A specific neural substrate for perceiving facial expressions of disgust. Nature 389: 495–498.

Phillips ML, Young AW, Scott SK, Calder AJ, Andrew C, Giampietro V, Williams SC, Bullmore ET, Brammer M, Gray JA (1998) Neural responses to facial and vocal expressions of fear and disgust. Proc R Soc Lond B Biol Sci 265: 1809–1817.

Puce A, Perrett D (2003) Electrophysiological and brain imaging of biological motion. Philosoph Trans Royal Soc Lond, Series B, 358: 435–445.

Ramachandran VS. Behavioral and magnetoencephalographic correlates of plasticity in the adult human brain. Proc Natl Acad Sci USA 1993; 90: 10413–20.

Ramachandran VS. Phantom limbs, neglect syndromes, repressed memories, and Freudian psychology. Int Rev Neurobiol 1994; 37: 291–333.

Ramachandran VS. Plasticity and functional recovery in neurology. Clin Med 2005; 5: 368–73.

Ramachandran VS, Hirstein W. The perception of phantom limbs. The D. O. Hebb lecture. Brain 1998; 121: 1603–30.

Ramachandran VS, Rogers-Ramachandran D, Cobb S. Touching the phantom limb. Nature 1995; 377: 489–90.

Ramachandran VS, Rogers-Ramachandran D. Phantom limbs and neural plasticity. Arch Neurol 2000; 57: 317–20.

Ramachandran VS, Rogers-Ramachandran D. It's all done with mirrors. Sci Am Mind 2007; 18: 16–9.

Ramachandran VS, Rogers-Ramachandran D. Sensations referred to a patient's phantom arm from another subjects intact arm: perceptual correlates of mirror neurons. Med Hypotheses 2008; 70: 1233–4.

Ramachandran VS, Rogers-Ramachandran D, Stewart M. Perceptual correlates of massive cortical reorganization. Science 1992; 258: 1159–60.

Rizzolatti G, Craighero L (2004) The mirror-neuron system. Annu Rev Neurosci 27: 169–192.

Rizzolatti G, Fogassi L, Gallese V (2001) Neurophysiological mechanisms underlying the understanding and imitation of action. Nature Rev Neurosci 2:661–670.

Rock I, Victor J. Vision and touch: an experimentally created conflict between the two senses. Science 1964; 143: 594–6.

Rose'n B, Lundborg G. Training with a mirror in rehabilitation of the hand. Scand J Plast Reconstr Surg Hand Surg 2005; 39: 104–8.

Royet JP, Plailly J, Delon-Martin C, Kareken DA, Segebarth C (2003) fMRI of emotional responses to odors: influence of hedonic valence and judgment, handedness, and gender. Neuroimage 20: 713–728.

Rozin R Haidt J and McCauley CR (2000) Disgust. In: Lewis M, Haviland-Jones JM (eds) Handbook of Emotion. 2nd Edition. Guilford Press, New York, pp 637–653.

Saxe R, Carey S, Kanwisher N (2004) Understanding other minds: linking developmental psychology and functional neuroimaging. Annu Rev Psychol 55: 87–124.

S. J. Russell and P. Norvig, Artificial intelligence: a modern approach (3rd edition): Prentice Hall, 2009.

Schienle A, Stark R, Walter B, Blecker C, Ott U, Kirsch P, Sammer G, Vaitl D (2002) The insula is not specifically involved in disgust processing: an fMRI study. Neuroreport 13: 2023–2026.

Showers MJC, Lauer EW (1961) Somatovisceral motor patterns in the insula. J Comp Neurol 117: 107–115.

Singer T, Seymour B, O'Doherty J, Kaube H, Dolan RJ, Frith CD (2004) Empathy for pain involves the affective but not the sensory components of pain. Science 303: 1157–1162.

Smith A (1759) The theory of moral sentiments (ed. 1976). Clarendon Press, Oxford.

S. N. Bose (1924). "Plancks Gesetz und Lichtquantenhypothese". Zeitschrift für Physik. 26 (1): 178–181.

Sprengelmeyer R, Rausch M, Eysel UT, Przuntek H (1998) Neural structures associated with recognition of facial expressions of basic emotions Proc R Soc Lond B Biol Sci 265: 1927–1931.

Strafella AP, Paus T (2000) Modulation of cortical excitability during action observation: a transcranial magnetic stimulation study. NeuroReport 11: 2289–2292.

Simonsen R (2015) Eating for the future: veganism and the challenge of in vitro meat. In: Stapleton P, Byers A (Hg). Biopolitics and utopia. Palgrave Macmillan, New York (2015), S 167–190

Tanaka K (1996) Inferotemporal cortex and object vision. Ann Rev Neurosci. 19: 109–140.

Tesla N. "My Inventions", 1919

T. R. Society, "Machine learning: the power and promise of computers that learn by example," ed. The Royal Society, 2017.

Tomasello M, Call J (1997) Primate cognition. Oxford University Press, Oxford.

Tremblay C, Robert M, Pascual-Leone A, Lepore F, Nguyen DK, Carmant L, Bouthillier A, Theoret H (2004) Action observation and execution: intracranial recordings in a human subject. Neurology. 63: 937–938.

Umilta MA, Kohler E, Gallese V, Fogassi L, Fadiga L, Keysers C, Rizzolatti G (2001) "I know what you are doing": a neurophysiological study. Neuron 32: 91–101.

Von Wright G.H., (1963), Norm and Action. A Logical Inquiry, Routledge & Kegan Paul, London.

Von Wright G.H., (1976), "Determinism and the Study of Man", in Essays on Explanation and Understanding, ed. by J. Manninen and R. Tuomela, Reidel, Dordrecht.

Von Wright G.H., (1977), "What is Humanism?", The Lindlay Lecture, University of Arkansas, Lawrence, Kansas.

Von Wright G.H., (1979), "Humanism and the Humanities", in Philosophy and Grammar, ed. by S. Kanger and S. Öhman, Reidel, Dordrecht, pp. 1-16. Reprinted in von Wright (1993).

Von Wright G.H., (1980), Freedom and Determination, North-Holland Publishing Co., Amsterdam.

Von Wright G.H., (1985), Of Human Freedom, The Tanner Lectures on Human Values,

Vol. VI, ed. by S. M. McMurrin, University of Utah Press, Salt Lake City, pp. 107-70. Reprinted in von Wright (1998).

Von Wright G.H., (1993), The Tree of Knowledge and Other Essays, Brill, Leiden.

Von Wright G.H., (1997), "Progress: Fact and Fiction", in The Idea of Progress, ed. by A. Burgen et al., W. de Gruyter, Berlin, pp. 1-18.

Von Wright G.H., (1998), In the Shadow of Descartes: Essays in the Philosophy of Mind, Kluwer, Dordrecht.

159

9 798552 354122